ALL ABOUT...

CHRISTMAS

Over 100 amazing facts behind the Christmas story

Written by
Alison Mitchell

Design by
André Parker

the**good**book
COMPANY

ALL ABOUT CHRISTMAS

The very first Christmas is one of the most famous stories in the world. But it's also a very old story, from around 2,000 years ago. So how do we know if it's true? And what are the facts behind it?

This book jumps into the Bible books of **Matthew** and **Luke** to discover what they tell us about the things that happened during that first Christmas. It includes Bible quotes so that we can read the story in their own words, and there's lots of help with any tricky words or phrases. It also explores what life was like for people at this time, especially those living in Israel as part of the Roman Empire. And we discover that God made amazing promises about a new King he was going to send—a Rescuer King who would save and lead his people. That's the King we celebrate every Christmas.

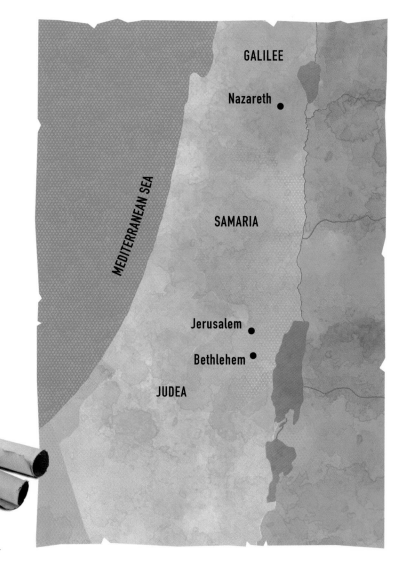

GALILEE

Nazareth

MEDITERRANEAN SEA

SAMARIA

Jerusalem

Bethlehem

JUDEA

All About: Christmas | © The Good Book Company 2022

thegoodbook.com | thegoodbook.co.uk | thegoodbook.com.au | thegoodbook.co.nz | thegoodbook.co.in

Design by André Parker | All photos licensed from iStock.com

ISBN: 9781784987763 | Printed in India

Contents

ABRAHAM	DAVID	BIRTH OF JESUS	TODAY
Around 4,000 years ago	Around 3,000 years ago	Probably between 7 BC and 4 BC	21st century

THE FIRST CHRISTMAS

The very first Christmas happened more than 2,000 years ago. So how do we know about it, and who told us?

Meet Matthew

The New Testament part of the Bible starts with four books called the Gospels. They are biographies of Jesus that were written by **Matthew, Mark, Luke** and **John**. Two of them—Matthew and Luke—begin with the Christmas story. When Matthew was writing his Gospel, he squeezed in loads of chunks from the Old Testament. Why? Because the Old Testament is full of promises about a new King. Matthew shows us that Jesus is this promised King.

A statue of Matthew from a church in Italy. He wouldn't have looked much like this!

When was Jesus born?

Do you know when Jesus was born? The answer may surprise you. The Bible doesn't tell us the date Jesus was born, or even the time of year, but he was almost certainly not born on December 25th. *December 25th* was chosen a very long time ago as a day to celebrate Jesus being born.

Choose your own birthday

Queen Elizabeth II was born in April 1926, but she has an "official birthday" on the second Saturday in June, which gives people in the UK a chance to celebrate in the warmth of summer. In a similar way, you can think of December 25th as Jesus' "official birthday".

The monk who got his arithmetic wrong

Dionysius was a monk who lived from about AD 470 to AD 544. We don't know exactly why, but he decided that the Roman consul at the time, Probius Junior, was consul exactly 525 years after Jesus was born. Because of his calculations, a new calendar using BC and AD was created. This calendar put the birth of Jesus at AD 1.

Oops

BUT Dionysius got his sums wrong. The Jewish king Herod the Great died in 4 BC, and we know that Herod was alive when Jesus was born. For that reason, most scholars put the birth of Jesus as being between 7 BC and 4 BC.

So Jesus was born "Before Christ"!

Calendars

The word "calendar" comes from the Latin term *calendarium*, which means "account book", because accounts were settled on the first day of the month. This Latin word comes from *calendae*, which was the Roman name for the first day in a month.

BC and AD

Dates are marked according to how long before or after the birth of Jesus they are. Dates before Jesus are marked "BC" meaning "Before Christ". Dates after Jesus are "AD" which stands for "Anno Domini", meaning "in the year of the Lord".

HOW LUKE STARTS HIS STORY

As well as Matthew (see pages 4-5), the other Bible writer who tells us about the first Christmas is Luke.

Meet Dr Luke*

*He probably didn't look anything like this!

Luke was a doctor who wrote two books about Jesus. His first book is called Luke's Gospel and is the life of Jesus. The word "Gospel" means Good News. Luke tells us the good news about who Jesus is and why he came.

Luke's second book is the book of Acts. It tells us about the first followers of Jesus. They believed that Jesus was the Christ (God's chosen King), so they were given a nickname—Christians. People who follow Jesus are still called Christians today.

Luke chapter 1 verses 1-4

¹ Many have undertaken to draw up an account of the things that have been fulfilled among us,

² just as they were handed down to us by those who from the first were eye witnesses and servants of the word.

³ With this in mind, since I myself have carefully investigated everything from the beginning, I too decided to write an orderly account for you, most excellent Theophilus, ⁴ so that you may know the certainty of the things you have been taught.

Theophilus

This name means someone who loves God. Luke was writing his book for everyone who loves to discover more about God.

Are you sure?

Luke wanted his friend, Theophilus, to be sure that the things he had been taught were true. So Luke wrote everything down so that his friend could be certain he knew the truth about Jesus.

Oral history

Luke tells us that the true stories in his book had been "handed down" by eye witnesses. These were people who saw these things for themselves. To start with, the stories about Jesus would have been passed on from one person to another by speaking and being memorised. This is called oral history and it is the way we know many of the things we have learned from long ago.

Qumran Caves

This is where the Dead Sea Scrolls were found between 1946 and 1956. They included very early copies of many Bible books.

Later, people like Luke wrote these stories onto scrolls. These scrolls were then copied by hand by scribes. These scribes were very, very careful not to make mistakes. They even counted the exact number of words, and then the number of letters, to be sure they had made a perfect copy. (And if they found a mistake, they had to throw their copy away and start again!)

Are you an investigator?

Do you like finding things out? Luke tells us that he "carefully investigated everything from the beginning" (v 3). That means he spoke to people to find out what they knew. He probably travelled around to ask as many people as possible. And then he wrote "an orderly account" so that we could learn all the same things that Luke learned.

This book you are reading now is full of facts about the first Christmas. It will help you to "carefully investigate" everything too!

Bible words (in blue)

- fulfilled (v 1): came true

- the word (v 2): the message about God

PROMISES FROM LONG AGO

A very long time ago God made some exciting promises to send a special new King. This King would rescue his people and then rule for ever and ever. The promises are written down for us in the Bible. You can also find some of them on this page.

A promise to Abraham

About 4,000 years ago God made some amazing promises to Abraham. This is one of them:

"All peoples on earth will be blessed through you." (Genesis 12 v 3)

This meant that someone from Abraham's family would be God's way of blessing (bringing good to) the whole world. That person was Jesus, who was born into Abraham's family about 2,000 years later.

A promise about Jesse

"A shoot will come up from the stump of Jesse; from his roots a Branch will bear fruit." (Isaiah 11 v 1)

Jesse is part of Jesus' family tree. He was the father of King David—the best king the Israelites ever had. Jesse and his family lived in Bethlehem, the same town Jesus would be born in 1,000 years later. Jesus was the "shoot" from Jesse's family.

What is a Jesse tree?

A Jesse tree is a traditional way of celebrating Advent. Each day, a symbol is hung on the tree as a reminder of Jesus' family tree and of people who were part of the Christmas events. There are three kinds of people on a Jesse tree:

1. Members of Jesus' family (starting with Adam)

2. Old Testament prophets who spoke about Jesus hundreds of years before he was born

3. People who met Jesus during the first Christmas

A promise to David

David was the first member of his family to become king of Israel. But God promised that a much greater King would come from David's family—someone who would be King for ever and ever.

"Your house and your kingdom shall endure for ever before me; your throne shall be established for ever."
(2 Samuel 7 v 16)

David didn't know who God meant when he made this promise, but we do—it's Jesus!

BELIEVING GOD'S WORDS

The Bible tells us that God always speaks the truth and that his promises always come true. But sometimes people find it hard to believe God's words. Zechariah was one of those people.

An unexpected meeting

Zechariah was a priest who served in God's temple in Jerusalem. One amazing day, the angel Gabriel appeared to Zechariah and told him that he and his wife, Elizabeth, were going to have a baby. But they were much too old, so Zechariah didn't believe it...

A model of the temple in Jerusalem where Zechariah was serving.

Luke chapter 1 verses 18-20

18 Zechariah asked the angel, "How can I be sure of this? I am an old man and my wife is well on in years."

19 The angel said to him, "I am Gabriel. I stand in the presence of God, and I have been sent to speak to you and to tell you this good news. 20 And now you will be silent and not able to speak until the day this happens, because you did not believe my words, which will come true at their appointed time."

Did Gabriel look like this? Head over to page 12 to find out more about angels...

Who is Gabriel?

The angel Gabriel was sent by God to tell Zechariah and Elizabeth they would have a baby. Later, Gabriel was also sent to tell someone else she would have a baby. That person was Elizabeth's relative—Mary.

?

Nine months later

Elizabeth did become pregnant, and nine months later she had a baby boy. But for all those months Zechariah couldn't say anything at all! Until eight days after the baby was born...

Luke chapter 1 verses 62-64

[62] Then they made signs to his father, to find out what he would like to name the child. [63] He asked for a writing tablet, and to everyone's astonishment he wrote, "His name is John." [64] Immediately his mouth was opened and his tongue set free, and he began to speak, praising God.

River Jordan

John was called "the Baptist" because he baptised people in the River Jordan as a sign that they had turned back to God.

John who?

Their baby son, John, grew up to be known as **John the Baptist.** Hundreds of years before, God had promised to send a messenger to his people to tell them to get ready for the promised Rescuer King (Isaiah 40 v 3). John grew up to be that messenger (Matthew 3 v 1-6). The name John means "gift of God". John was God's gift to his people to help them to get ready for Jesus.

Bible words (in blue)

- angel (v 19): special messenger sent by God

- appointed time (v 20): the time God has chosen

- writing tablet (v 63): a clay tablet covered with a layer of wax so that people could write on the soft wax surface with a pointed stylus

ALL ABOUT ANGELS

Angels pop up a lot in the Bible. But what are they? And why do they appear?

Meet the messengers

Angels are spiritual beings who serve God. During the first Christmas, God sent angels as his messengers to spread the good news about the coming of his Son, Jesus. The angel Gabriel had unexpected messages for Elizabeth and for Mary; then later a large group of angels popped up with some wonderful news for the shepherds.

But God doesn't usually send angels to speak to us! Instead, God speaks to us when we read his words in the Bible. That's how we discover the message about Christmas now.

Myth-busting

Have you seen pictures like these? A cute blonde angel sitting on a cloud and playing a harp? That's nothing like the angels we meet in the Bible! Instead, Bible angels are more like warriors. Most of them look like men—not women or children—and only some of them have **wings**.

Bible facts about angels

Angels are mentioned at least **273** times in the Bible. We discover that they were created by God (Colossians 1 v 16), they live for ever (Luke 20 v 36), they were there when God created the world (Job 38 v 1-7), they can fly (Daniel 9 v 21), there are thousands of them (Hebrews 12 v 22), and they get very excited when someone becomes a Christian (Luke 15 v 7)!

Seraphim and cherubim

Some angels are called seraphim. The Old Testament book of Isaiah tells us that seraphim each have "six wings: with two wings they covered their faces, with two they covered their feet, and with two they were flying" (Isaiah 6 v 2). Also, you may have heard a cute baby described as a cherub. But real cherubim are warrior angels. Two of them were sent to guard the entrance to the garden of Eden so that no one could go in (Genesis 3 v 24). There were also statues of two cherubs covering the ark of the covenant (Exodus 25).

Sssss

This is called a jumping spider, and is actually quite cute!

What are you scared of?

Which of these are you scared of? Spiders? Snakes? The dark?

How about angels?! Surprisingly, every time someone meets an angel in the Bible they are terrified! So the first thing the angel needs to say is "don't be afraid".

AN AMAZING MESSAGE FOR MARY

Six months after telling Zechariah that he and Elizabeth would have a baby, the angel Gabriel visited a teenager called Mary with the astonishing news that she was going to have a special baby too.

Luke chapter 1 verses 30-38

30 But the angel said to her, "Do not be afraid, Mary, you have found favour with God. 31 You will conceive and give birth to a son, and you are to call him Jesus. 32 He will be great and will be called the Son of the Most High. The Lord God will give him the throne of his father David, 33 and he will reign over Jacob's descendants for ever; his kingdom will never end."

34 "How will this be?" Mary asked ...

35 The angel answered, "The Holy Spirit will come on you, and the power of the Most High will overshadow you. So the holy one to be born will be called the Son of God. 36 Even Elizabeth your relative is going to have a child in her old age, and she who was said to be unable to conceive is in her sixth month. 37 For no word from God will ever fail."

38 "I am the Lord's servant," Mary answered. "May your word to me be fulfilled." Then the angel left her.

This is a famous statue of King David by the artist Michelangelo. The real David probably wore more clothes...

King for ever

Jesus came from David's family line, and would be King for ever, just as God had promised to David 1,000 years earlier (see pages 8-9).

Never ending...

Throughout history, kingdoms have come and gone. Ancient Egypt lasted for around 3,000 years. Rome was the capital of an empire for around 700 years. In today's world there is a mix of kings, queens, presidents and prime ministers. But none of them last for ever. Only Jesus—the King of kings—has a kingdom that will never end!

Who's the father?

All babies are special, but this baby was different from any other. His mother was Mary; but his father was God. So Jesus was totally human and also totally God. Mind-blowing—but true!

Never failing

God's words are always right and good. His promises never fail to come true. So we can always trust what God says.

Bible words (in blue)

- conceive (v 31): become pregnant

- the Most High (v32, 35): a title for God

- descendants (v 33): children, grandchildren, great-grandchildren and so on

- overshadow (v 35): in a way we don't fully understand, God's Holy Spirit came over Mary and she became pregnant

- fulfilled (v 38): come true

DAILY LIFE

What was it like living in Israel at the time of the first Christmas?

Housing

Houses were made of either clay bricks or stones and had dirt floors. Many families lived in one-room houses, which had steps up the outside so that the roof could also be used as living space. Inside the house, a raised platform at one end gave a place to eat and sleep, while the lower part was often used as a stable.

Playing outside

Children also played a game similar to hopscotch.

Toys and games

Toys from those days that have been found by archaeologists include whistles, rattles, toy animals on wheels, hoops and spinning tops.

Off to work

Tradesmen used to wear symbols to show what kind of work they did. For example, tailors stuck needles in their tunics and carpenters tucked wood chips behind their ears. Other common jobs for men included being farmers or fishermen. Women mostly worked at home, looking after the house and cooking for their families.

Roman occupation

Jesus was born at the time of Caesar Augustus, the first emperor of Rome. The country of Israel was part of the huge Roman Empire, meaning that the Romans were in charge. The people living in Israel longed to have their country back under their own control. (See pages 24-25 for more about the Roman occupation.)

PAGE 24

Honey

To make one pound (450 grams) of honey, bees must collect nectar from around 2 million flowers.

Favourite food

Today, much of our favourite food has been processed, with ingredients already put together and ready to eat. But in New Testament times everything had to be made from scratch. Meat was a luxury, though there was plenty of **fish**, which could be eaten fresh or dried to eat later. A typical meal would be **vegetables** and **bread**, and maybe some **nuts**, **honey** or **cheese**.

What did people wear?

Clothing was much simpler than today and mostly made from wool or linen. Both men and women wore a tunic, tied with a fabric belt (which was sometimes also used as a purse). Women's tunics were ankle-length, whereas working men would have shorter tunics finishing just below the knee. Only very rich men wore long tunics. When cold, or at night, a cloak could be worn over the tunic. People were either barefoot or wore sandals made of leather or wood. People living in Israel had olive-toned skin and dark hair.

Wool from sheepskin can be spun into a long strand using a wooden spindle, and then woven into warm clothing.

MARY VISITS ELIZABETH

When Elizabeth was six months pregnant, her relative Mary came to visit her.

Luke chapter 1 verses 39-45

[39] At that time Mary got ready and hurried to a town in the hill country of Judea, [40] where she entered Zechariah's home and greeted Elizabeth. [41] When Elizabeth heard Mary's greeting, the baby leaped in her womb, and Elizabeth was filled with the Holy Spirit. [42] In a loud voice she exclaimed:

"Blessed are you among women, and blessed is the child you will bear! [43] But why am I so favoured, that the mother of my Lord should come to me?

[44] "As soon as the sound of your greeting reached my ears, the baby in my womb leaped for joy. [45] Blessed is she who has believed that the Lord would fulfil his promises to her!"

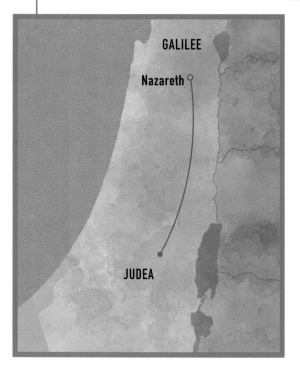

Cross-country

Mary lived in a small town called Nazareth, which was in Galilee in the country of Israel. Her relative, Elizabeth, lived in another part of Israel called Judea. Mary's journey was about 80 miles.

How did Elizabeth know?

Mary hadn't had time to tell Elizabeth her news yet, so how did Elizabeth know that Mary was going to have a special child? Verse 41 tells us that Elizabeth was "filled with the Holy Spirit". The Holy Spirit points people to Jesus. That's how Elizabeth knew that Mary was to be Jesus' mother.

Stages of pregnancy

Elizabeth was "in her sixth month" (Luke 1 v 36) when Gabriel told Mary that she would have a baby too. A typical pregnancy lasts for around **nine months** (from 37 to 42 weeks).

This period is divided into trimesters, with each one lasting for three months. Elizabeth was at the end of her second trimester.

Jumping for joy

From around the fifth month of pregnancy, mothers can feel their babies moving inside them. When Elizabeth saw Mary, she felt her baby jumping for joy inside her.

!?

Bible words (in blue)

- Holy Spirit (v 41): The Holy Spirit is God. Every Christian has the Holy Spirit with them all the time, helping them to live for God.

- blessed (v 42): given good things by God

- favoured (v 43): chosen, preferred

SINGING AT CHRISTMAS

When she arrived at Elizabeth's home, Mary was so full of joy that she started to sing: "My soul glorifies the Lord and my spirit rejoices in God my Saviour" (Luke 1 v 46-47). People have sung at Christmastime ever since.

Silent Night

The words for this carol were written in 1816 by an Austrian priest called Father Joseph Mohr. He wrote the carol in German, with the title "Stille Nacht". The music was added in 1818 by a school teacher called Franz Xaver Gruber. The music was originally played on a guitar, with an organ arrangement added a few years later.

Nearly 100 years later, British and German soldiers were fighting during World War 1. They agreed on a truce for a few hours on Christmas Day 1914. This was the carol they sang together, as it was one they all knew. Some sang it in English—"Silent Night, Holy Night...", and some in German, "Stille Nacht, Heilige Nacht..."

SILENT NIGHT, HOLY NIGHT

Silent Night, Holy Night!
Guiding Star shine ever bright
While the Eastern Magi bring
Gifts and homage to our King.
Peace, goodwill to men!

Silent Night, Holy Night!
May we know thy delight,
And with Angels may we sing
Glory to the newborn King.
Peace, goodwill to men!

An early printing press from 1901

*Did you know that it was Gutenberg's invention that made the very first printed Bible possible? Known as the Gutenberg Bible, it was printed in Mainz in Germany in 1455.

Hark! The Herald Angels Sing

At first, this tune had nothing to do with Christmas. It was written by the famous composer Felix Mendelssohn in 1840, as part of a piece of music celebrating the inventor of the printing press, Johannes Gutenberg*. But in the 1850s, the tune was matched with a 1739 poem by the hymnwriter Charles Wesley, and the hymn as we know it was born.

What was the first Christmas carol?

One of the first carols was "Angels Hymn" from AD 129. It was around this time that people started to sing Christian-themed hymns to replace pagan songs that had been sung at a time known as the winter solstice.

One of the oldest printed carols is the "Boar's Head Carol", first printed in 1521. It is thought to have been sung while Christmas lunch was carried in. Other carols from the Middle Ages include "God Rest You Merry, Gentlemen" and "While Shepherds Watched Their Flocks by Night".

What makes carols sound Christmassy?

Carols will often have a stirring melody that also includes some minor chords, so that you hear a mix of major and minor melodies. That kind of music fits well with words that are celebratory but also thoughtful. Some instruments associated with Christmas would include organs, trumpets and sleigh bells.

What's wassailing?

In the 19th century, groups of singers started to meet in public spaces to sing carols to the passers-by. This became known as wassailing, and has continued ever since.

Mary's song

Mary's song is sometimes known as the "Magnificat", because in a Bible translated into Latin (the language the Romans spoke), that's the first word of the song. It is still sung in churches today as a reminder of some of the great things God did by sending Jesus, his Son.

JOSEPH'S NIGHT-TIME SURPRISE

Joseph was engaged to Mary. But while he was asleep, an angel popped up with an astounding message.

Matthew chapter 1 verses 18-21

18 This is how the birth of Jesus the Messiah came about: his mother Mary was pledged to be married to Joseph, but before they came together, she was found to be pregnant through the Holy Spirit. 19 Because Joseph her husband was faithful to the law, and yet did not want to expose her to public disgrace, he had in mind to divorce her quietly.

20 But after he had considered this, an angel of the Lord appeared to him in a dream and said, "Joseph son of David, do not be afraid to take Mary home as your wife, because what is conceived in her is from the Holy Spirit. 21 She will give birth to a son, and you are to give him the name Jesus, because he will save his people from their sins."

Who was Matthew?

Matthew wrote one of the four Gospels (biographies of Jesus). He was writing for Jewish readers who would know the Old Testament really well. So Matthew included lots of Old Testament quotes in his Gospel. There's more about Matthew on pages 4-5.

PAGES 4-5

Jesus the Messiah/Christ

Messiah (a Greek word) and **Christ** (the same word in Hebrew) both mean "**the anointed one**". This is a way of saying that Jesus is God's chosen King.

They look like this in their original languages:

Χριστος

Greek for "Christ"

חישמה

Hebrew for "Messiah"

What does the name Jesus mean?

Jesus means "God saves". It tells us who Jesus is—he is **God**; and it tells us what Jesus does—he **saves** his people.

What is sin?

Sin means not loving God or treating him as King, so that we do what *we* want instead of what *he* wants. The result of sin is that we can't be friends with God and enjoy life with him for ever. You can see why Jesus needs to save us from our sins!

O come, o come, Immanuel

Later in Matthew's Gospel we discover another name for Jesus. He is called Immanuel, which means "God with us" (Matthew 1 v 23). When Jesus was born it meant that God was with his people as a human being. He was totally human. And totally God too. Awesome!

Bible words (in blue)

- pledged (v 18): promised

- Holy Spirit (v 18): The Holy Spirit is God. See page 19 to find out more.

- divorce (v 19): even though Joseph and Mary weren't married yet, breaking their engagement was seen as divorce (separating two people due to be married)

- son of David (v 20): Joseph was part of King David's family line

- conceived (v 20): made pregnant

THE ROMAN EMPIRE

At the time Jesus was born, Israel was part of the mighty **Roman Empire**. Jerusalem, the capital of Israel, had been captured by the Roman general Pompey in 63 BC. The Romans occupied Israel for around 400 years. The people of Israel knew that God had promised to send the Messiah, a King who would rescue them. They hoped this King would save them from the Romans.

Did you know?
The names of all our months have Roman origins. **August** is named after **August**us Caesar.

The Roman army

The Romans had the largest and most feared army in the ancient world. Their soldiers could march for 20 miles a day, while carrying a pack that weighed 90lb (40kg) or more. The army was divided into legions, with each legion having 4,000 to 6,000 soldiers. A legion was further divided into centuries, with 80 men in each one. The man in charge of a century was a centurion. Only Roman citizens could become legionaries (the professional foot soldiers) but every legion was also supported by auxiliary soldiers, often from the countries occupied by the Roman Empire.

Emperors

Rome wasn't always ruled by emperors. For around 500 years Rome had been a republic, until that ended in a civil war. The war started when a general called **Julius Caesar** seized power. After he was killed, his adopted son, Octavian, won a series of huge battles until he became the sole ruler—the first emperor. At that point he changed his name to **Caesar Augustus**. Rome was ruled by emperors for the next 500 years.

Heads or tails?

The first living Roman to have his head on a coin was Julius Caesar.

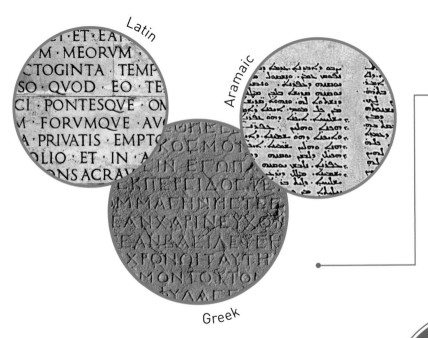

Latin

Aramaic

Greek

Local languages

The language of ancient Rome was Latin, but many countries also had their own languages or dialects. In New Testament Israel, the commonly spoken language was Aramaic. The New Testament part of the Bible, which includes the accounts of the first Christmas, was written in a third language: Greek.

Roman worship

In the early empire, Romans worshipped lots of gods and goddesses. They even made some of their emperors into "gods". This made things hard for the early Christians, who refused to worship an emperor as a god. Some Christians were put to death for believing in Jesus Christ. But in the 4th century AD, the emperor Constantine made Christianity the official religion of the empire.

Colosseum

It is thought that some Christians were killed by lions in the Colosseum in Rome, but the records from the time aren't clear.

THE BIRTH OF JESUS CHRIST

Luke tells us that Joseph and Mary had to travel to Bethlehem before Jesus was born. Luke also tells us what an unlikely item the baby had for a crib!

Luke chapter 2 verses 1-7

[1] In those days Caesar Augustus issued a decree that a **census** should be taken of the entire Roman world. [2] (This was the first census that took place while Quirinius was governor of Syria.) [3] And everyone went to their own town to register.

[4] So Joseph also went up from the town of Nazareth in Galilee to Judea, to **Bethlehem** the town of David, because he belonged to the house and line of David. [5] He went there to register with Mary, who was pledged to be married to him and was expecting a child. [6] While they were there, the time came for the baby to be born, [7] and she gave birth to her **firstborn**, a son. She wrapped him in **cloths** and placed him in a **manger**, because there was no guest room available for them.

?

A long journey

Joseph and Mary travelled from Nazareth to Bethlehem. That's 80 miles (130km): a very long way to walk, especially when pregnant. An old Christmas tradition says that Mary rode on a donkey, but the Bible doesn't tell us how they travelled. Maybe Joseph found a cart for Mary to sit in. Or perhaps they just walked very slowly...

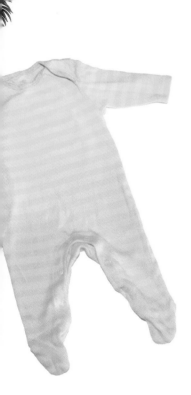

Clothing for babies

Today we keep babies warm and comfortable in special clothing—maybe like this babygro. In New Testament times, babies were wrapped in strips of cloth for the same reason. These are sometimes known as **swaddling clothes.**

Swaddling a baby was common practice—but it wasn't only baby boys and girls who were wrapped in swaddling clothes. Sometimes baby lambs would be swaddled as well, to keep them clean and safe. The lambs born in the fields near to Bethlehem may have been destined to be taken to the Jerusalem Temple as sacrifices. Only perfect, undamaged lambs were good enough for the temple. Perhaps this is a hint that this baby had come as a "lamb", to die as a sacrifice to make people friends with God (read John 1 v 29).

What is a manger?

A manger is a box where food for animals was kept. But this manger was different! Instead of holding food for animals, this manger held the baby Jesus.

Was Jesus born in a stable?

Probably not. The Bible never says Jesus was born in a stable—just that he slept in a manger. In those times people often brought their animals in overnight to keep them safe. That would be in the downstairs part of someone's home. There would be a manger there in case the animals were hungry. So Jesus was probably born downstairs in someone's home.

Bible words (in blue)

- census (v 1): official count of people

- firstborn (v 7): first child

WHO'S IN CHARGE?

At this point in the story the two most powerful people seem to be Caesar Augustus and King Herod the Great. But who was *really* in charge?

Who was King Herod the Great?

At the time Jesus was born, Judea (the south of Israel) was ruled by Herod the Great. He was famous for big building projects, including the Jerusalem Temple, and also for being so scared that someone would take over his throne that he had several members of his own family murdered! It's no surprise that Herod was worried when he heard rumours about a new "King of the Jews". Herod didn't want anyone to be king except himself.

Israel was part of the Roman Empire, so Herod was a "puppet king". This means he couldn't always do what he wanted because the Romans were "pulling his strings".

CENSUS!

Census

An official count or survey, often to find out exactly who is living in a country or area.

Herod's Temple
Known as the Second Temple, it was started in around 19 BC and destroyed by the Romans in AD 70.

Who was Caesar Augustus?

The Bible tells us that "in those days Caesar Augustus issued a decree that a **census** should be taken of the entire Roman world" (Luke 2 v 1).

Augustus was the first Roman emperor. He became emperor after his uncle, Julius Caesar, died, and he ruled from 27 BC until his death in AD 14. He was known for bringing two centuries of peace to the Roman Empire, known as the *Pax Romana*—though his own rise to power was anything but peaceful!

It seems likely that Augustus ordered more than one census while he was emperor. One of them happened at the time of Jesus' birth, and it meant that Joseph and Mary had to travel to Bethlehem. While they were there, Jesus was born (Luke 2 v 6).

A Roman helmet, worn by Roman soldiers or "legionaries".

Why was Jesus born in Bethlehem?

Was the Roman census the only reason Jesus was born in Bethlehem? No! Hundreds of years beforehand, this is what God said:

> "But you, Bethlehem Ephrathah,
>   though you are small among the clans of Judah,
> out of you will come for me
>   one who will be ruler over Israel,
> whose origins are from of old,
>   from ancient times." (Micah 5 v 2)

So the Romans ended up doing what God had always said would happen. King Herod wasn't in charge. The Romans weren't in charge. It was God who decided what would happen and where. God is the Real King. He is the one in charge!

SHEPHERDS AND ANGELS

Luke tells us about some shepherds in the hills outside Bethlehem. They were about to get a great shock...

Luke chapter 2 verses 8-20

8 And there were shepherds living out in the fields near by, keeping watch over their flocks at night. 9 An angel of the Lord appeared to them, and the glory of the Lord shone around them, and they were terrified. 10 But the angel said to them, 'Do not be afraid. I bring you good news that will cause great joy for all the people. 11 Today in the town of David a Saviour has been born to you; he is the Messiah, the Lord. 12 This will be a sign to you: you will find a baby wrapped in cloths and lying in a manger.'

13 Suddenly a great company of the heavenly host appeared with the angel, praising God and saying,

14 'Glory to God in the highest heaven,

and on earth peace to those on whom his favour rests.'

15 When the angels had left them and gone into heaven, the shepherds said to one another, 'Let's go to Bethlehem and see this thing that has happened, which the Lord has told us about.'

16 So they hurried off and found Mary and Joseph, and the baby, who was lying in the manger. 17 When they had seen him, they spread the word concerning what had been told them about this child, 18 and all who heard it were amazed at what the shepherds said to them. 19 But Mary treasured up all these things and pondered them in her heart. 20 The shepherds returned, glorifying and praising God for all the things they had heard and seen, which were just as they had been told.

All true
Everything the angels told the shepherds was true.

Fat tails

Sheep need to be kept safe both day and night, so these shepherds lived in the fields with their flocks. The most common variety of sheep was fat-tailed sheep. The fat in the tail provides energy reserves in harsh climates (a bit like a camel's hump).

Shepherds

Many of the shepherds in the fields around Bethlehem were Levitical shepherds. They followed the laws in the Old Testament book of Leviticus (see page 27). These laws explained how a lamb must be kept perfect for sacrifice in the Jerusalem Temple.

Check it out

The shepherds checked that what the angels had said was true. That's what this book does too—checking the facts behind the Christmas story.

Christians

Christians do what the shepherds did: they check the facts in the Bible and then tell other people (v 17); and they also do what Mary did: they treasure the truths about Jesus (v 19).

CHRISTMAS TRADITIONS

The events of the first Christmas happened over 2,000 years ago. Since then, people around the world have celebrated the birth of Jesus. Here are a few of the ways people enjoy Christmas today.

Iceland – The Yule Lads

In the 13 nights before Christmas, Icelandic children put their shoes by the window and wait to be visited by the Yule Lads. Each morning, they will either find sweets/candies in their shoes (if they have been good) or rotten potatoes!

There's a little [...] hiding somew[...] these pages. C[...] find it?!

Germany – Find the pickle

As well as lights and ornaments, Germans like to hide a pickle somewhere on the Christmas tree. The child who finds it gets an extra gift.

Venezuela – Roller skates

In Caracas, the capital of Venezuela, people head to church in the early morning on Christmas Eve. But they don't walk. They go on roller skates. This tradition is so popular that the roads are closed to cars so that people can safely roller-skate to church.

Ukraine – Spiders' webs

An old Ukrainian folktale says that a poor widow couldn't afford to decorate a tree for her children. So the spiders in her house decorated it with sparkling webs instead. Even today, Ukrainians put decorations that look like **webs** on their Christmas trees.

New Zealand – Christmas in summer

In New Zealand, Christmas is in the summer, so many of their traditions centre around a barbecue or a beach. They use the **Pohutukawa** as a Christmas tree, as it has bright red flowers in December.

Japan – KFC

Back in 1975, the American fast-food chain Kentucky Fried Chicken launched a marketing campaign in Japan. The slogan was "Kurisumasu ni wa kentakkii!", which means "Kentucky for Christmas". It was so popular that many Japanese families still have a KFC meal on Christmas Eve.

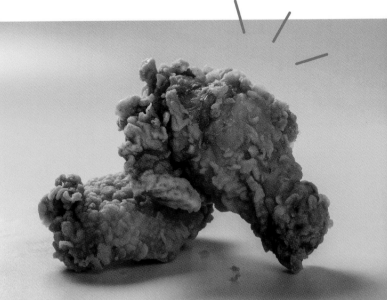

South Africa – Christmas caterpillars

What's your favourite Christmas food? Roast turkey? Mince pies? How about fried caterpillars?! In South Africa, families enjoy a plate of special caterpillars, from the Pine Tree Emperor Moth, also known as the Christmas caterpillar.

WAITING FOR JESUS

Joseph and Mary took the baby Jesus to the temple in Jerusalem to thank God for their son. Inside the temple courts they met two old people who had been waiting to meet Jesus...

Luke chapter 2 verses 26-32

26 It had been revealed to [Simeon] by the Holy Spirit that he would not die before he had seen the Lord's Messiah. 27 Moved by the Spirit, he went into the temple courts. When the parents brought in the child Jesus to do for him what the custom of the Law required, 28 Simeon took him in his arms and praised God, saying:

29 "Sovereign Lord, as you have promised,
   you may now dismiss your servant in peace.
30 For my eyes have seen your salvation,
31 which you have prepared in the sight of all nations:
32 a light for revelation to the Gentiles,
   and the glory of your people Israel."

FOMO

Do you have a "bucket list" of things you want to do? Do you worry about FOMO (Fear Of Missing Out)? Simeon knew there was only one thing he needed to see before he died—the promised Rescuer King! Nothing else mattered compared to that.

Salvation time

Thousands of years before Jesus was born, God had promised to send a new King who would save his people. As soon as Simeon saw the baby, he knew that Jesus was the promised Rescuer King. No wonder Simeon thanked and praised God!

Look for this ring on page 23 to find out about Jesus' name...

Who did the King come for?

The people of Israel had been God's people in the Old Testament. His promise of a Rescuer King was for them. But not just for them. God showed Simeon that this rescue was for non-Jews (Gentiles) as well. God's amazing rescue was offered to everyone everywhere! That includes every single person reading this page. Wow!

Meet Anna

Anna was very old. She loved God and lived in his temple. Like Simeon, Anna was waiting for God to keep his promise to save his people (redemption).

Luke chapter 2 verses 36-38

36 There was also a prophet, Anna, the daughter of Penuel, of the tribe of Asher. She was very old; she had lived with her husband seven years after her marriage, 37 and then was a widow until she was eighty-four. She never left the temple but worshipped night and day, fasting and praying. 38 Coming up to them at that very moment, she gave thanks to God and spoke about the child to all who were looking forward to the redemption of Jerusalem.

Twelve tribes

The Israelites were divided into twelve tribes, named after the sons of Jacob (Exodus 1 v 1-5). The map shows where each tribe settled when the Israelites first moved into the land God had promised them. Which tribe did Anna come from (Luke 2 v 36)? Can you spot it on the map?

Bible words (in blue)

- Lord's Messiah (v 26): God's promised Rescuer King

- custom of the Law (v 27): God's Old Testament law told people how to thank God for their first child

- Gentiles (v 32): non-Jews

- prophet (v 36): God's messenger

- fasting (v 37): going without food for a time to concentrate on worshipping God

HERE COME THE MAGI

Some of Jesus' visitors were from nearby, such as the shepherds, but others came from much further away...

Matthew chapter 2 verses 1-8

¹ After Jesus was born in Bethlehem in Judea, during the time of King Herod, Magi from the east came to Jerusalem ² and asked, "Where is the one who has been born king of the Jews? We saw his star when it rose and have come to worship him."

³ When King Herod heard this he was disturbed, and all Jerusalem with him. ⁴ When he had called together all the people's chief priests and teachers of the law, he asked them where the Messiah was to be born. ⁵ "In Bethlehem in Judea," they replied, "for this is what the prophet has written:

⁶ "'But you, Bethlehem, in the land of Judah,
   are by no means least among the rulers of Judah;
for out of you will come a ruler
   who will shepherd my people Israel.'"

⁷ Then Herod called the Magi secretly and found out from them the exact time the star had appeared. ⁸ He sent them to Bethlehem and said, "Go and search carefully for the child. As soon as you find him, report to me, so that I too may go and worship him."

PAGE 28

Bible words (in blue)

- Magi (v 1): wise men
- disturbed (v 3): troubled, worried

Watch out for Herod

Check back to page 28 to find out what Herod did to his own family. Do you think the wise men could trust him?

An old, old story

You may have heard a traditional story that says that these visitors were kings called Melchior, Belthazar and Caspar. But Matthew doesn't say that. He just calls them "Magi from the east". He doesn't say they are kings. He doesn't tell us their names. He doesn't even say there were three of them. There could just as easily have been four visitors—and we might choose to call them Fred, Ned, Jed and Ted!

Why doesn't Matthew tell us more about these visitors? Because the details don't matter. What really matters is that these men knew that Jesus was God's promised Rescuer King—and so they had "come to worship him" (v 2).

3?

Camels

The Bible doesn't tell us that the wise men rode camels, but this would have been a good way to travel across the wilderness from the east to Bethlehem.

O Little Town of Bethlehem

In verse 6 the religious leaders are quoting one of God's Old Testament promises to send the Rescuer King. You can find some of those promises on pages 8-9. Which other famous king came from the town of Bethlehem?* He pops up quite a lot in this book.

*King David came from Bethlehem.

STAR FOLLOWERS

The word "Magi" can be translated as magicians, astrologers or simply "wise men". So how wise were these visitors? They knew the stars well enough to spot a new one when it appeared—and wisely follow wherever it went.

Matthew chapter 2 verses 9-12

9 After they had heard the king, [the Magi] went on their way, and the star they had seen when it rose went ahead of them until it stopped over the place where the child was. 10 When they saw the star, they were overjoyed. 11 On coming to the house, they saw the child with his mother Mary, and they bowed down and worshipped him. Then they opened their treasures and presented him with gifts of gold, frankincense and myrrh. 12 And having been warned in a dream not to go back to Herod, they returned to their country by another route.

How old was Jesus?

You may have seen Christmas cards that show the wise men visiting a stable, but that may not have been what happened. We know from what Herod does next that Jesus is likely to have been a toddler by now, maybe as old as two. So it may well be that the wise men were visiting the house where the young Jesus was living with Mary and Joseph— still in Bethlehem, but not a stable.

God always knows

As we will see next, Herod had lied to the Magi. He didn't want to worship Jesus—he wanted to murder him! But God always knows what people are thinking. So he warned the Magi not to trust Herod, and they went home another way.

Some facts about stars

If you look up at the night sky, without a telescope, how many stars do you think you can see? (*Answer at bottom of page.) Did you know that every star you can see is actually bigger and brighter than our sun? Wow! They just look smaller because they are so much further away.

There is a bright star called Deneb, in the constellation Cygnus, that can be seen from most parts of the world. It is at least 19,000,000,000,000,000 miles away (that's 19 quadrillion miles)!

Deneb is at least 50,000 times brighter than the sun.

Bible words (in blue)

- gold, frankincense and myrrh (v 11): precious gifts fit for a king. Frankincense is a tree resin that smells beautiful when burned. Myrrh is a fragrant spice or oil that was put on dead bodies to prepare them for burial.

*If there is no moon and no streetlights, you may be able to see around 2,000 to 2,500 stars. Imagine trying to count them!

ANGEL WARNINGS

King Herod had a secret plan to murder Jesus—but God knew all about it so he warned the wise men not to go back to Herod. Check out the gold words to see what else God did to keep Jesus safe:

Matthew chapter 2 verses 13-23

13 When [the wise men] had gone, an angel of the Lord appeared to Joseph in a dream. "Get up," he said, "take the child and his mother and escape to Egypt. Stay there until I tell you, for Herod is going to search for the child to kill him."

14 So he got up, took the child and his mother during the night and left for Egypt …

16 When Herod realised that he had been outwitted by the Magi, he was furious, and he gave orders to kill all the boys in Bethlehem and its vicinity who were two years old and under …

19 After Herod died, an angel of the Lord appeared in a dream to Joseph in Egypt 20 and said, "Get up, take the child and his mother and go to the land of Israel, for those who were trying to take the child's life are dead."

21 So he got up, took the child and his mother and went to the land of Israel. 22 … Having been warned in a dream, he withdrew to the district of Galilee, 23 and he went and lived in a town called Nazareth. So was fulfilled what was said through the prophets, that he would be called a Nazarene.

Herod fails

King Herod was a murderer. He even killed some of his own family because he thought they might be planning to become king instead of him. But he couldn't kill Jesus. Why not? Because God was always in control. He knew what Herod was planning and he kept Jesus safe.

God wins

Herod wasn't just trying to kill a young child, horrible though that is. He was also trying to stop God's plans. And nobody can ever do that! God had promised that he would send a Rescuer King. And nobody and nothing could stop that promise from coming true. God always wins!

Dreaming of angels

Joseph had seen an angel in a dream before (see pages 22-23). This time, God sent his angel to tell Joseph how to keep Jesus safe.

Bible words (in blue)

- vicinity (v 16): nearby area
- withdrew (v 22): went away
- Nazarene (v 23): someone from Nazareth in Galilee

WHAT HAPPENED NEXT?

Christmas is a time when we celebrate Jesus, the Rescuer King, being born. But what happened when Jesus grew up?

The greatest storyteller

We've whizzed forward 30 years to when Jesus was an adult. He told wonderful stories (called parables) that showed people what it was like to live in God's kingdom. This one is about a rescue...

Luke chapter 15 verses 4-7

4 Suppose one of you has a hundred sheep and loses one of them. Doesn't he leave the ninety-nine in the open country and go after the lost sheep until he finds it? 5 And when he finds it, he joyfully puts it on his shoulders 6 and goes home. Then he calls his friends and neighbours together and says, "Rejoice with me; I have found my lost sheep." 7 I tell you that in the same way there will be more rejoicing in heaven over one sinner who repents than over ninety-nine righteous people who do not need to repent.

Shepherd searching

Can you imagine a shepherd losing a sheep and then saying "I don't care"? No way! He will search high and low until he finds his lost sheep. Then he will pop it on his shoulders, carry it safely home—and have a party to celebrate.

So precious...

Imagine losing something that is very precious to you. Maybe a game you love, a toy you've had since you were little, or your best pair of sneakers. How would you feel? And how hard would you look for the thing you had lost? In the story of the lost sheep, Jesus says that people are even more precious to God. He doesn't want anyone to be lost.

Angel party

"Rejoicing in heaven" (v 7) means that the angels have a party when someone is rescued by Jesus. Wow!

The point of a parable

Jesus' parables weren't just good stories—they were designed to make you think carefully. This one isn't really about woolly animals, or the human shepherds who look after them. It's about people—and their perfect Shepherd.

How can people be lost?

Like a stupid sheep, people wander away from God. They live their own way instead of God's way. The Bible calls this sin, and tells us that sin stops us being friends with God. That's why God sent his Rescuer King. Jesus rescues everyone who trusts in him. He saves us from our sin and makes it possible for us to be God's friends. Wow! You can see why the angels have a party when a sinner puts their trust in Jesus!

Bible words (in blue)

- sinner (v 7): someone who doesn't live God's way
- repents (v 7): turns away from doing wrong
- righteous (v 7): right with God

QUIZ TIME

This book has over 100 amazing facts behind the Christmas story. How many can you remember? Try this quiz to find out—but be warned, some of them are trick questions!

1 When was Jesus probably born?

    a) In the year AD 1

    b) Between 7 BC and 4 BC

    c) Around AD 5

2 Thousands of years ago, God told some people about his promise to send a new King. What did God say about this King?

    a) He would be King for ever.

    b) He would rescue his people.

    c) He would be part of King David's family.

3 How did God tell Zechariah, Mary and Joseph about the new King?

    a) By text

    b) By a letter

    c) By an angel

4 What is usually the first thing an angel says?

    a) Good morning

    b) Don't be afraid

    c) My name is Gabriel

5 Which carol was sung by British and German soldiers on Christmas Day 1914?

    a) Silent Night

    b) O Come All Ye Faithful

    c) Hark! The Herald Angels Sing

6 What does the name Jesus mean?

    a) God saves

    b) King of kings

    c) King for ever

7 Who is the month of August named after?

    a) Augustus Caesar

    b) Augustus Gloop

    c) Augustus John

8 Joseph and Mary travelled from Nazareth to Bethlehem before Jesus was born. How far is that?

    a) 60 miles / 100km

    b) 80 miles / 130km

    c) 100 miles / 160km

9 The baby Jesus was wrapped in swaddling clothes. What else was sometimes swaddled?

a) Baby elephants

b) Baby lambs

c) Baby goats

10 How do people travel to church on Christmas Eve in Caracas, Venezuela?

a) On bicycles

b) On scooters

c) On roller skates

11 What was Simeon waiting for?

a) His supper

b) His Saviour

c) His slippers

12 How many Magi were there?

a) Three

b) Four

c) We don't know

13 How did God keep Jesus safe from King Herod?

a) He warned the wise men not to go back to Herod.

b) He sent an angel to warn Joseph.

c) He told Joseph to take Mary and Jesus to Egypt.

14 Who was the most powerful ruler during the first Christmas?

a) King Herod

b) Augustus Caesar

c) The Lord God

8. b (p 26-27)

7. a (p 24-25)

6. a. Jesus means "God Saves."—but he is also the King of kings and King for ever! (p 23)

5. a (p 20-21)

4. b (p 13)

3. c (p 10, 14, 22)

2. All of them are true! (p 8-9)

1. b (p 4-5)

14. c. Every page shows that God is always in control – wow!

13. God did all of these. He made sure that Jesus would be safe. (p 38, 40)

12. c (p 36-37)

11. b (p 34-35)

10. c (p 32-33)

9. b (p 26-27)

GLOSSARY

Abraham
God promised Abraham that his family would become a huge nation. They were called the Israelites. Abraham lived around 2,000 years before Jesus was born.

AD
Dates after Jesus are marked "AD", which stands for "Anno Domini", meaning "in the year of the Lord".

Advent
Means "arrival". The weeks leading up to Christmas look forward to the time when we celebrate the arrival of Jesus.

Angels
Supernatural beings sent by God as his messengers.

BC
Dates before Jesus are marked "BC", which means "Before Christ".

Bethlehem
A town in the south of Israel, where Jesus was born. Bethlehem was also the birthplace of King David.

Bible
The word "Bible" means "books". The Bible is God's word to us. There are 66 books in the Bible.

Caesar Augustus
Roman emperor at the time Jesus was born.

Christ
A Greek word meaning "the anointed one". When someone was crowned as king, they had oil poured on them (anointed). So the title "Christ" shows that Jesus is God's chosen (anointed) King. The same word in Hebrew is "Messiah".

Christian
A Christian is someone who has put their trust in Jesus Christ, and who loves and follows him.

Christmas
Means "mass on Christ's day". A mass is a religious celebration, so Christmas is the day we celebrate the birth of Jesus Christ.

David
David was the best king the Israelites ever had. God promised David that someone from his family would be King for ever. That someone was Jesus.

Elizabeth
Mary's relative.

Gabriel
An angel sent by God to both Mary and Elizabeth.

Gospels
The word "gospel" means "good news". There are four Gospels in the New Testament part of the Bible, written by Matthew, Mark, Luke and John. All of the Gospels tell us the good news about Jesus. Two of them—Matthew and Luke—include the events of the first Christmas.

Herod the Great
Herod was the king of Judea in the south of Israel at the time Jesus was born.

Holy Spirit
There is one God, but he is three persons: God the Father, God the Son (Jesus), and God the Holy Spirit. The Holy Spirit points people to Jesus.

Immanuel
This title for Jesus means "God with us".

Israel
Jesus was born and lived in the country of Israel. He was born in the south, in Bethlehem, and grew up in the north, in Nazareth.

Jerusalem
The capital city of Israel. Herod's temple was in Jerusalem.

Jesse
King David's father. God had promised that his Rescuer King—Jesus—would come from Jesse's family line.

Jesus
The name Jesus means "God saves". It tells us who he is—Jesus is God—and what he does—Jesus saves his people.

Joseph
Mary's husband.

Luke
Wrote one of the four Gospels telling us the "good news" (gospel) about Jesus. Luke tells us that he very carefully checked with eyewitnesses before writing (Luke 1 v 1-4).

Magi
Wise men.

Manger
An animal's food box.

Mary
Chosen by God to be the mother of Jesus. Jesus' father was God himself!

Matthew
Wrote one of the four Gospels. Matthew wrote especially for Jewish people and therefore included lots of quotes from the Old Testament.

Messiah
Messiah (Hebrew) and Christ (Greek) are the same word in different languages. See "Christ" above for what this title means.

Nazareth
A town in the north of Israel where Jesus grew up.

New Testament
There are 27 books in the New Testament part of the Bible. They tell us about Jesus and his followers, and what it means to live for him.

Old Testament
The 39 books of the Old Testament form the oldest part of the Bible. They tell us about the time before Jesus was born, and include lots of promises that Jesus was coming.

Priest
Someone who served God. Elizabeth's husband, Zechariah, was a priest.

Prophet
The Old Testament prophets gave people messages from God. Some of those messages told God's people that he had promised to send a Rescuer King.

Sacrifice
A way of saying thank you or sorry to God. Sacrifices in the Jerusalem Temple included the death of an animal (such as a lamb) or a gift of money.

Saviour
Someone who saves or rescues us. God promised thousands of years ago to send a Rescuer King. Jesus is that Saviour.

Sin
Sin means not loving God or treating him as King, so that we do what we want instead of what he wants. The result of sin is that we can't be friends with God and enjoy life with him for ever.

Swaddling clothes
Strips of cloth wrapped around a baby to keep him or her clean and warm.

Temple
God's temple in Jerusalem reminded his people that he was with them. People went there to pray, to offer sacrifices, and to give thanks to God.

Worship
Showing by what we do that God is the greatest. Worship can include praying and singing, as we thank God for his goodness, and also living the way God wants us to live.

Zechariah
Elizabeth's husband, who saw the angel Gabriel in the temple.